E. B. White

Rennay Craats

www.av2books.com

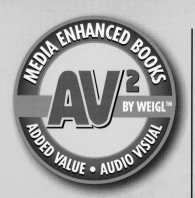

AV² provides enriched content that supplements and complements this boo Weigl's AV² books strive to create inspired learning and engage young mir in a total learning experience.

Your AV² Media Enhanced books come alive with...

Audio
Listen to sections of the book read aloud.

Key Words
Study vocabulary, and complete a matching word activity.

Video
Watch informative video clips.

Quizzes
Test your knowledge.

Go to **www.av2books.com**, and enter this book's unique code.

BOOK CODE

V94352

Embedded Weblinks
Gain additional information for research.

Slide Show
View images and captions, and prepare a presentation.

AV² by Weigl brings you media enhanced books that support active learning.

Try This!
Complete activities and hands-on experiments.

... and much, much mor

Published by AV² by Weigl
350 5th Avenue, 59th Floor
New York, NY 10118

Website: www.weigl.com www.av2books.com
Copyright ©2014 AV² by Weigl

Library of Congress Cataloging-in-Publication Data

Craats, Rennay.
 E. B. White / Rennay Craats.
    pages cm. -- (Remarkable Writers)
 Includes index.
 ISBN 978-1-62127-405-6 (hardcover : alk. paper) -- ISBN 978-1-62127-411-7 (softcover : alk. paper)
 1. White, E. B. (Elwyn Brooks), 1899-1985--Juvenile literature. 2. Authors, American--20th century--Biography--Juvenile literature. 3. Children's stories--Authorship--Juvenile literature. I. Title.
 PS3545.H5187Z617 2014
 818'.5209--dc23
 [B]
                        2012040832

Printed in the United States of America, in North Mankato, Minnesota
1 2 3 4 5 6 7 8 9 0 16 15 14 13

012013
WEP301112

Senior Editor: Heather Kissock
Design: Terry Paulhus

Weigl acknowledges Getty Images and Alamy as its primary photo suppliers for this title.

Contents

Introducing E. B. White

G rowing up would not be the same without the wonderful tales by author Elwyn Brooks White, better known as E. B. White. Children love to read about Stuart Little's adventures, Charlotte's clever plans to save Wilbur the pig, and Louis the swan's trumpet playing. E. B. White's children's books are classics. They are read in schools and homes across the country.

At the beginning of his career, children were not E. B.'s main readers. He made a living writing essays for adults that were published in newspapers and magazines. He also wrote popular books of poetry. E. B. began writing children's stories to entertain his son, nieces, and nephews. His stories, which amused his family, also delighted millions of young readers around the world. E. B. White's stories are timeless.

E. B. White began his writing career in journalism before becoming a children's writer.

Today, many of his early fans have grown up. Many are still reading E. B. White's books—to their own children. E. B. wrote only three children's novels during his writing career. Those three books have made him a legend in children's **literature**.

🐭 Stuart Little is one of E. B. White's best-known characters. The little mouse has been featured in television shows and movies.

Writers are often inspired to record the stories of people who lead interesting lives. The story of another person's life is called a biography. A biography can tell the story of any person, from authors such as E. B. White, to inventors, presidents, and sports stars.

When writing a biography, authors must first collect information about their subject. This information may come from a book about the person's life, a news article about one of his or her accomplishments, or a review of his or her work. Libraries and the internet will have much of this information. Most biographers will also interview their subjects. Personal accounts provide a great deal of information and a unique point of view. When some basic details about the person's life have been collected, it is time to begin writing a biography.

As you read about E. B. White, you will be introduced to the important parts of a biography. Use these tips and the examples provided to learn how to write about an author or any other remarkable person.

Early Life

Of Samuel and Lillian White's six children, Elwyn Brooks White was the youngest. E. B. was born on July 11, 1899, in Mount Vernon, New York. His father was the owner of a piano manufacturing company. The Whites' large farmhouse was filled with love and happiness. However, this did not always keep young E. B. from worrying. From the darkness of the attic to his future, E. B. worried about everything.

"Some writers for children deliberately avoid using words they think a child doesn't know. But children are game for anything. I throw them hard words, and they backhand them over the net."
—*E. B. White*

One of E. B.'s greatest fears was of public speaking. When he was a young student, everyone who attended E. B.'s school had to present a poem or a speech in front of an audience. E. B. worried about reading his assignment aloud. He thought the other students would laugh at him. At times, E. B.'s fear of public speaking was so great that he would just run off the stage. E. B. would try to coax other students into reading his poems and speeches in his place. The fear of public speaking never left E. B. White.

Mount Vernon is located in the southern part of New York State. It is a suburb of New York City.

Growing up on a farm, E. B. was happiest when he was near animals. He took care of chickens' eggs and enjoyed watching baby chicks hatch. His dog, Mac, was never far from his side. E. B. often kept to himself. He liked to ride his bicycle, ice-skate, and canoe. He also liked to write. E. B. found it exciting to fill blank pages with his own words. It was then that E. B. overcame one of his biggest fears—not knowing what he would do for a living. He decided to become a writer.

E. B. was a good writer. When he was 11 years old, he wrote a poem about a mouse. The poem was published in a magazine. The following year, E. B.'s story "A Winter Walk" received top honors in a writing contest. It was published in *St. Nicholas Magazine*, a children's journal. Whenever E. B. had spare time, he wrote poems and stories. They were about his life, his views of the world, and about animals. E. B. continued to be fascinated by these subjects for the rest of his life.

Writing About Early Life

A person's early years have a strong influence on his or her future. Parents, teachers, and friends can have a large impact on how a person thinks, feels, and behaves. These effects are strong enough to last throughout childhood, and often a person's lifetime.

In order to write about a person's early life, biographers must find answers to the following questions.

1 Where and when was the person born?

2 What is known about the person's family and friends?

3 Did the person grow up in unusual circumstances?

As a child, E. B. White loved animals. It is not surprising that he wrote books about them.

Growing Up

Although E. B. White was a good student, he was motivated by more than just a love of learning. E. B. worked hard at school, partly out of fear. He was afraid of attracting the teachers' attention and of falling behind his classmates in his studies. In high school, E. B. wrote essays about local news and political issues for the school magazine. He also filled the role of assistant editor.

In high school, E. B. wrote essays about local and worldly issues for the school magazine.

Meanwhile, Europe was on the brink of World War I. E. B. thought the United States should not go to war. Many of his essays expressed this opinion. In 1914, World War I began, and the United States supported the **Allies**. Although he was against his country's involvement, E. B. remained **patriotic**. He wanted to support his country. E. B. was too young to become a soldier, so he supported the war effort by working on farms belonging to farmers who were serving overseas. E. B. joined the army in 1918. He served as a private before returning to New York to attend Cornell University in Ithaca.

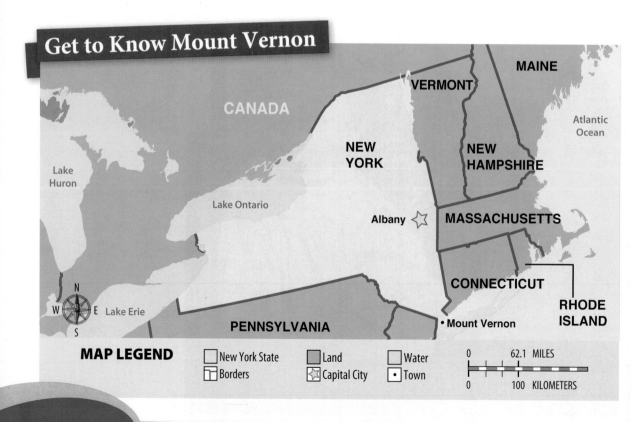

Get to Know Mount Vernon

MAINE

VERMONT

CANADA

Atlantic Ocean

NEW YORK

NEW HAMPSHIRE

Lake Huron

Lake Ontario

Albany ☆ MASSACHUSETTS

N
W · E   Lake Erie
S

CONNECTICUT

RHODE ISLAND

• Mount Vernon

PENNSYLVANIA

MAP LEGEND
☐ New York State
⊟ Borders
☐ Land
⊠ Capital City
☐ Water
⊡ Town

0   62.1 MILES
0   100 KILOMETERS

In E. B. White's first year at Cornell University, he wrote for the university newspaper. Since he had not yet outgrown his shyness, E. B. thought that joining a **fraternity** might help him become bolder, and it did. His fraternity brothers called him Andy because he had the same last name as the school's president, Andrew White. The name stuck, and people called him Andy for the rest of his life. E. B. was elected president of his fraternity in his junior year at Cornell University. Despite his popularity, E. B. did not forget about his writing. He was named head editor of the university's daily newspaper.

William Strunk, Jr., an English professor at Cornell University, taught E. B. how to craft his writing. William Strunk, Jr. is best known for his writer's guidebook *The Elements of Style*. E. B. graduated from Cornell University in 1921. By that time, he had written more than 180 **editorials** for the university newspaper.

🖉 E. B. White enjoyed Cornell University so much that he wrote an essay entitled "I'd Send My Son to Cornell." Much later, E. B.'s son did attend Cornell University.

Some people know what they want to achieve in life from a very young age. Others do not decide until much later. In any case, it is important for biographers to discuss when and how their subjects make these decisions. Using the information they collect, biographers try to answer the following questions about their subjects' paths in life.

1 Who had the most influence on the person?

2 Did he or she receive assistance from others?

3 Did the person have a positive attitude?

Developing Skills

After he graduated, E. B. felt that he was ready to tackle the "real world," but settling down was not as easy as he thought. E. B. and a school friend, Howard Cushman, decided to travel for a while. E. B. gathered a few things and packed them into his automobile. Without a fixed destination or very much money, the two started driving across the United States. They wrote short articles for magazines along the way and found odd jobs to pay for gas and food. E. B. and Howard worked on farms, played piano, and washed dishes to fund their travels. They ended up in Seattle, Washington, and E. B. decided to stay there. He found a job reporting for the *Seattle Times*, where he worked for one year.

> "What am I saying to my readers? Well, I never know. Writing to me is not an exercise in addressing readers, it is more as though I were talking to myself while shaving."
> —*E. B. White*

E. B.'s next adventure was a six-week cruise to Alaska. He could not afford the trip, so he found a job working in the ship's **mess hall**. When the trip was over, E. B. returned home to focus on his writing career.

Seattle is the largest city in the U.S. Northwest. More than three million people live in the city and its surrounding area.

At the age of 22, E. B. returned to the state of New York and moved in with his parents. He was not sure where to look for writing jobs. A **literary** magazine called *The New Yorker* caught E. B.'s eye when it first came to newsstands. He admired the quality of writing, so he began submitting articles. Within a few months, *The New Yorker* began publishing his articles. Before long, people all over the country were reading his words.

Over the next forty years, E. B. became an important part of *The New Yorker*. He wrote essays, poems, stories, and news pieces. While working for *The New Yorker*, E. B. met and fell in love with the magazine's editor, Katharine Angell. They were married in 1929. Two years later, they had a son, Joel. Seven years after that, the Whites moved to a farm in Maine. In Maine, E. B. continued to write for *The New Yorker* and other literary magazines.

꙳ Although E. B. and his wife, Katharine, worked together at *The New Yorker*, she never edited E. B. 's writing. He would not let her see his work until it was finished.

Writing About Developing Skills

Every remarkable person has skills and traits that make him or her noteworthy. Some people have natural talent, while others practice diligently. For most, it is a combination of the two. One of the most important things that a biographer can do is to tell the story of how the subject developed his or her talents.

1 What was the person's education?

2 What was the person's first job or work experience?

3 What obstacles did the person overcome?

Timeline of E. B. White

1899

Elwyn Brooks White is born on July 11, in Mount Vernon, New York.

1929

E. B. marries *The New Yorker* fiction editor Katharine Angell and publishes his first collection of poetry.

1911

E. B. wins a writing contest for his story "A Winter Walk," which is published in a children's journal.

1921

He graduates from Cornell University.

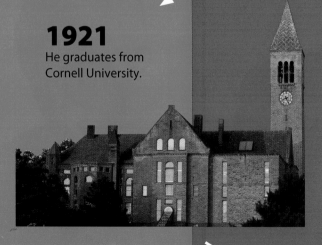

1926

E. B. joins the staff of *The New Yorker* magazine.

1938
E. B. White and his wife move to a farm in Maine.

1945
Stuart Little is published.

1952
Charlotte's Web is published.

1985
E. B. White dies after a lengthy battle with **Alzheimer's disease**.

1977
Katharine Angell White passes away.

1970
The Trumpet of the Swan is published.

Early Achievements

Although he was an **established** essay writer, E. B. had never thought about writing children's literature. He certainly did not consider himself to be a storyteller. However, his son Joel, and numerous nieces and nephews, began asking E. B. to tell them stories. He made up imaginative stories for them. The children would ask to hear their favorite stories again and again. Sometimes E. B. would forget some details of his stories. He starting writing them down to remember them.

E. B. White had never thought about writing children's literature. He did not consider himself to be a storyteller.

One of the characters in E. B.'s stories was a little mouse named Stuart Little. The amusing story idea came to E. B. while he was sleeping on a train. He did not write the tale until ten years later. Writing the story was more difficult than he thought it would be. It was a challenge for him to sit and write for long periods of time. However, E. B. kept working at it and finished the book in 1945. *Stuart Little* was a great success, making E. B. White a famous children's author.

The 1999 movie *Stuart Little* is based on E. B. White's well-loved book.

Over the years, E. B. continued to write **inspirational** books for children. In 1952, *Charlotte's Web* was published. It was a story about the friendship between a pig and a spider. E. B. spent several months researching spiders and animal behavior. He wanted to make the story believable and to get his characters just right. He based the book partly on his own experiences growing up on a farm, surrounded by animals. Once again, E. B.'s book was a great success. It earned him many awards and was translated into twenty different languages.

It was many years before children could begin reading a new E. B. White book. In 1970, he published *The Trumpet of the Swan*. E. B., who was a **perfectionist**, was not completely happy with the book. However, children and **critics** loved it. *The Trumpet of the Swan* earned E. B. several awards. Although he continued to write, *The Trumpet of the Swan* was his last children's novel.

The Trumpet of the Swan was made into a movie in 2001. It told the story through animation, or as a cartoon.

Writing About

Early Achievements

No two people take the same path to success. Some people work very hard for a long time before achieving their goals. Others may take advantage of a fortunate turn of events. Biographers must make special note of the traits and qualities that allow their subjects to succeed.

1 What was the person's most important early success?

2 What processes does the person use in his or her work?

3 Which of the person's traits were most helpful in his or her work?

Tricks of the Trade

While writing is not always easy, the results are worth it. E. B. White followed certain rules when he wrote. These tips can help you improve your writing, too.

Choice Words

As a young boy, E. B. spent a great deal of time flipping through the pages of his dictionary in search of great treasures—words. As an adult, he continued to improve his **vocabulary** by watching out for fascinating words. Words are the building blocks of any piece of writing. Having a good dictionary and using it is very important. Authors work hard to select the perfect word or to use an interesting word in place of a more common one.

Write in a Journal

People keep a journal or diary for many reasons. Some people want to keep a record of everything that happens to them. For other people, having a journal allows them to keep track of their thoughts and feelings. E. B. started writing in a journal when he was 8 years old. He filled its pages with the day's events. He also overcame many of his fears by writing about them.

ᴡ Reference books, including dictionaries, are a valuable tool for writers. They help writers use words and information properly.

Over and Over Again

The key to good writing is rewriting. This step occurs after the completion of the first **draft** of a story. Many authors will revise their writing several times to make improvements. Even E. B. White, who started writing before he was a teenager, had to revise his writing. In fact, he rewrote the beginning of *Charlotte's Web* nine times before he was happy with it. That is why many writers publish only one book every few years. For many writers, it can take a long time to put the finishing touches on a story.

> "I like animals, and my barn is a very pleasant place to be, at all hours!"
> —*E. B. White*

Write What You Know

One way to come up with an idea for a story is to draw from real-life experiences. This does not mean that the story has to be completely true. For new writers, it is often easier to write about a familiar subject. E. B. White wrote about what he knew and loved best. If he did not know much about a subject, he would research it thoroughly.

Comfort Level

Being comfortable can help one's ideas flow. Many writers follow a routine to ease themselves into their work. Some write at a certain time of day. Others require complete quiet or the sound of a radio playing softly in the background. Writers need to find out what routine works best for them. E. B. could write in the midst of noise and disruptions. Often, his children would run circles around his desk as he worked. However, E. B.'s work area was much like his writing style—clean and simple. E. B. kept his desk bare and set it near an open window. Keeping his desk clutter-free was important to him.

E. B. loved being around animals. It was natural for him to write stories using animals as characters.

Remarkable Books

For years, E. B. White's wonderful stories have thrilled young readers. His books are entertaining and enjoyable. This section will provide you with brief introductions to some of E. B.'s most-loved books and the characters found within those books.

Charlotte's Web

In this story of friendship and hardship, E. B. White reminds readers that even simple things, such as a barnyard, can be filled with wonder. *Charlotte's Web* is set on a farm. When a litter of pigs is born, the farm owner decides to kill the **runt**. He thinks that it will likely die anyway. The farmer's daughter, Fern, begs him to let her raise the piglet.

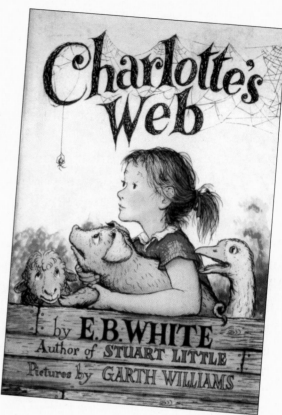

Fern calls the little pig Wilbur and nurses him from a bottle until he grows strong. Before long, Wilbur the pig is too big for Fern to care for. She sells Wilbur to her uncle, Homer Zuckerman. His farm is just down the street, so Fern can still visit her friend. Wilbur misses Fern, but he is not lonely for long. A spider named Charlotte lives in the doorway of Wilbur's new pigpen. She becomes his best friend. Wilbur soon adds geese, sheep, and a rat named Templeton to his list of barnyard friends. When Fern comes by to visit, she sits on a stool and listens to the animals' conversations.

The barnyard fun is soon hampered by a terrible discovery: Wilbur's new owner, Homer, is planning to serve him for Christmas dinner. Poor Wilbur is very afraid. He does not want to die. Charlotte promises to save Wilbur from the Christmas feast. Charlotte's clever plan to save Wilbur and the adventures that follow will keep readers on the edge of their seats.

AWARDS
Charlotte's Web
1953 Newbery Honor Book
1958 Lewis Carroll Shelf Award
1970 George C. Stone Center for Children's Books Recognition of Merit Award
1973 New England Round Table of Children's Libraries Award

Stuart Little

The Littles are a family with an extraordinary child. Their son, Stuart, is a mouse. Measuring only 2 inches (5 centimeters) tall, Stuart's small size leads him on many adventures. He is lowered into a bathtub drain to find a lost ring and chased by the family cat, Snowbell. Stuart even fixes the piano by squeezing himself between the key spaces. His size certainly does not stop him from having many great adventures. His greatest round of adventures begins when his best friend, a bird named Margalo, flies away from the Littles' home. Margalo flies away because she is afraid that she will be eaten by Snowbell. Stuart leaves home in search of his friend. His transportation is a miniature car, which has a real gasoline-powered motor in it. Stuart Little meets interesting characters while on his quest. Some of the characters help Stuart out of sticky situations, while others get him into even bigger messes.

AWARDS
Stuart Little
1970 Laura Ingalls Wilder Award

The Trumpet of the Swan

Louis is a trumpeter swan who cannot trumpet. One day, Louis meets Sam, a boy who tries to help him. Sam teaches Louis to communicate through reading and writing. Louis uses a chalkboard to write messages to those around him. Louis's father wants him to communicate with other swans as well. Although he knows his actions are wrong, Louis's father smashes the window of a music store and steals a trumpet. Louis learns to play the trumpet with great skill. Even though he is thankful for the trumpet, Louis feels guilty that his father stole it from the music store. He decides to find a job to pay back the owner of the music store. Louis has other plans, too. He wants to return home and win the heart of the beautiful female swan, Serena. This story is entertaining and fun, while teaching valuable life lessons.

AWARDS
The Trumpet of the Swan
1972 International Board on Books for Young People Honor List
1973 Children's Book Award
1973 Sequoyah Children's Book Award
1974 Sue Hefley Award from the Louisiana Association of School Librarians
1975 Young Hoosier Award

From Big Ideas to Books

W hen he sat down to write his first children's book, E. B. was already a well-known author. He spent many years thinking about the character Stuart Little before writing about the mouse's adventures. Finally, E. B. sent the completed **manuscript** to Harper & Row Publishers. The children's book editor of the company, Ursula Nordstrom, loved the story. She accepted the manuscript for publication. E. B. worked with artist Garth Williams on the illustrations for the book.

"I had been watching a big grey spider at her work and was impressed by how clever she was at weaving. Gradually I worked the spider into the story."
—E. B. White

Still, not everyone liked the book. The head of children's literature at the New York Public Library raised concerns about the book. She believed that *Stuart Little* was missing a tidy, happy ending. She felt children would be disappointed if the story was left **open-ended**. Some people also thought that the story was too unbelievable. Despite criticism, the book was published.

The Publishing Process

Publishing companies receive hundreds of manuscripts from authors each year. Only a few manuscripts become books. Publishers must be sure that a manuscript will sell many copies. As a result, publishers reject most of the manuscripts they receive. Once a manuscript has been accepted, it goes through

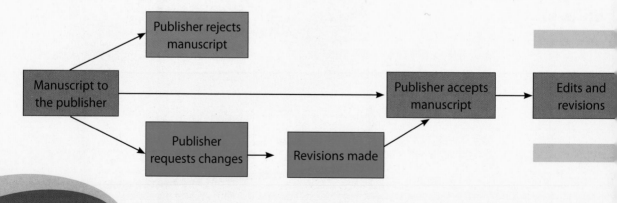

After the enormous success of *Stuart Little*, children and parents eagerly awaited E. B.'s next book. Even his publisher did not know that he was busy writing *Charlotte's Web*. E. B. had not discussed the book with anyone. One day, E. B. simply appeared at Harper & Row Publishers and handed Ursula an envelope. He left without saying a word. In the envelope was the manuscript for *Charlotte's Web*. Ursula could hardly believe how great the story was. After reading only a few chapters, she was convinced that E. B. had done it again.

Charlotte's Web was published in 1952. Today, it is known as one of the best children's books of all time. In 1970, *The Trumpet of the Swan* was published, much to the delight of E. B.'s loyal fans. Like his other two children's books, *The Trumpet of the Swan* quickly became a classic.

📖 E. B. White's writing was inspired by events that happened in his life. Wilbur, the pig in *Charlotte's Web*, is based on a pig E. B. White met. Like Wilbur, this pig was to be sent for slaughter.

many stages before it is published. Often, authors change their work to follow an editor's suggestions. Once the book is published, some authors receive royalties. This is money based on book sales.

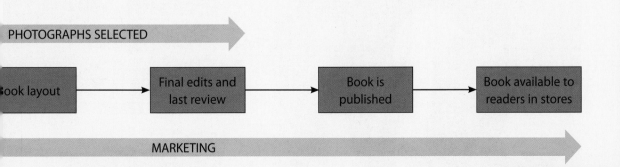

PHOTOGRAPHS SELECTED

Book layout → Final edits and last review → Book is published → Book available to readers in stores

MARKETING

E. B. White Today

Over the years, E. B. valued his privacy more and more. Sadly, Katharine Angell White died in 1977. After the loss of his wife, E. B. guarded his privacy. He rarely gave interviews and avoided award presentations. When he was given an award, he would send a written acceptance speech that the presenters could read to the crowd.

E. B. White rarely gave interviews and avoided award presentations.

When E. B. retired, he lived permanently on his farm in Maine. There, he focused on what mattered most to him. He took care of his farm animals, canoed, and spent time with his family. E. B. lived a quiet and simple life during his retirement. The great writer passed away on October 1, 1985. E. B. died from an illness called Alzheimer's disease. He was 86 years old.

📖 E. B. White's farmhouse in North Brooklin, Maine, was close to his family, including his grandchildren. This allowed them to spend time together.

The author's death saddened the entire nation. E. B.'s characters and stories touched adults and young people, not just in the United States, but around the globe. E. B.'s books had been an important part of growing up for many children. The author also inspired a great number of journalists and magazine writers, who remembered E. B. as the reason they started their writing careers. E. B. White delighted and inspired people all over the world.

E. B.'s death did not affect readers' interest in his books. Long after the books were first published, children and adults continue to read these classic tales. In 1990, a nation-wide poll of the United States found that *Charlotte's Web* was still named the favorite book among children. Today, E. B. White is remembered as a gifted essayist and a wonderful storyteller.

Writing About Person Today

The biography of any living person is an ongoing story. People have new ideas, start new projects, and deal with challenges. For their work to be meaningful, biographers must include up-to-date information about their subjects. Through research, biographers try to answer the following questions.

1 Has the person received awards or recognition for accomplishments?

2 What is the person's life's work?

3 How have the person's accomplishments served others?

E. B. White received many awards for his contributions to American literature over the years. In 1963, he was given the Presidential Medal of Freedom by President John F. Kennedy.

Fan Information

People who want to experience E. B. White's stories have many ways to do so. After reading the books, fans can listen to voice recordings of the stories. There are even some recordings done by E. B. White himself. E. B. White made a tape recording of *Charlotte's Web* in 1973. The author's stories have also appeared on the small and big screens. *Stuart Little* was made into a television movie in 1966. It was then released as a full-length movie in 1999. *Charlotte's Web* was made into a cartoon movie in 1972 and a film in 1973.

A new movie version of *Charlotte's Web* was released in 2006. It starred Dakota Fanning as Fern.

Readers who enjoy E. B. White's books can find more information about him on the internet. There are many websites that feature E. B.'s children's stories. Surfing the internet is a great way to learn about this gifted author.

📖 As well as being a cartoon, the 1973 film of *Charlotte's Web* was a musical. It featured several songs that helped to tell the story.

📖 The 1999 *Stuart Little* movie proved to be so popular that it spawned two sequels. *Stuart Little 2* was released in 2002. The third movie came out three years later.

Write a Biography

All of the parts of a biography work together to tell the story of a person's life. Find out how these elements combine by writing a biography. Begin by choosing a person whose story fascinates you. You will have to research the person's life by using library books and reliable websites. You can also e-mail the person or write him or her a letter. The person might agree to answer your questions directly.

Use a concept web, such as the one below, to guide you in writing the biography. Answer each of the questions listed using the information you have gathered. Each heading on the concept web will form an important part of the person's story.

Parts of a Biography

Early Life

Where and when was the person born?

What is known about the person's family and friends?

Did the person grow up in unusual circumstances?

Growing Up

Who had the most influence on the person?

Did he or she receive assistance from others?

Did the person have a positive attitude?

Developing Skills

What was the person's education?

What was the person's first job or work experience?

What obstacles did the person overcome?

Person Today

Has the person received awards or recognition for accomplishments?

What is the person's life's work?

How have the person's accomplishments served others?

Early Achievements

What was the person's most important early success?

What processes does the person use in his or her work?

Which of the person's traits were most helpful in his or her work?

Test Yourself

1 Where was E. B. White born?

2 How did E. B. White feel about speaking in public?

3 After he finished high school, what university did E. B. attend?

4 Who was the English professor who helped E. B. craft his writing?

5 Who did E. B. White marry?

6 For what national literary magazine did E. B. work?

7 What is the title of E. B.'s first children's book?

8 Where did E. B. White live during his retirement?

9 Did noise bother E. B. White when he was writing?

10 What is unique about the Littles' son, Stuart?

ANSWERS
1. E. B. White was born in Mount Vernon, New York. 2. E. B. had a great fear of public speaking. 3. Cornell University in Ithaca, New York 4. William Strunk, Jr. 5. Katharine Angell, editor of *The New Yorker* 6. *The New Yorker* 7. *Stuart Little* 8. E. B. stayed on his farm in Maine. 9. E. B. White had no problem working with noise in the background. 10. Stuart Little is a mouse.

Writing Terms

This glossary will introduce you to some of the main terms in the field of writing. Understanding these common writing terms will allow you to discuss your ideas about books and writing with others.

action: the moving events of a work of fiction

antagonist: the person in the story who opposes the main character

autobiography: a history of a person's life written by that person

biography: a written account of another person's life

character: a person in a story, poem, or play

climax: the most exciting moment or turning point in a story

episode: a short piece of action, or scene, in a story

fiction: stories about characters and events that are not real

foreshadow: hinting at something that is going to happen later in the book

imagery: a written description of a thing or idea that brings an image to mind

narrator: the speaker of the story who relates the events

nonfiction: writing that deals with real people and events

novel: published writing of considerable length that portrays characters within a story

plot: the order of events in a work of fiction

protagonist: the leading character of a story; often a likable character

resolution: the end of the story, when the conflict is settled

scene: a single episode in a story

setting: the place and time in which a work of fiction occurs

theme: an idea that runs throughout a work of fiction

Key Words

Allies: the nations that fought against the Central Powers in World War I

Alzheimer's disease: a brain disorder that affects memory

critics: people whose job it is to say or write their opinions

draft: a first, rough version of a piece of writing

editorials: articles in a newspaper, usually expressing the author's point of view

established: settled into a respectable position in one's business

fraternity: an organization made up of male university or college students

inspirational: something that serves to motivate

literary: relating to writing and books

literature: writing of lasting value, including plays, poems, and novels

manuscript: a draft of a story before it is published

mess hall: the place where the ship's crew eat in close quarters

open-ended: having no fixed answer or conclusion

patriotic: supporting and defending one's country and its interests

perfectionist: a person who demands a standard of excellence

runt: an undersized animal

vocabulary: all of the words used or understood by a person or group

Index

Log on to www.av2books.com

AV² by Weigl brings you media enhanced books that support active learning. Go to www.av2books.com, and enter the special code found on page 2 of this book. You will gain access to enriched and enhanced content that supplements and complements this book. Content includes video, audio, weblinks, quizzes, a slide show, and activities.

AV² Online Navigation

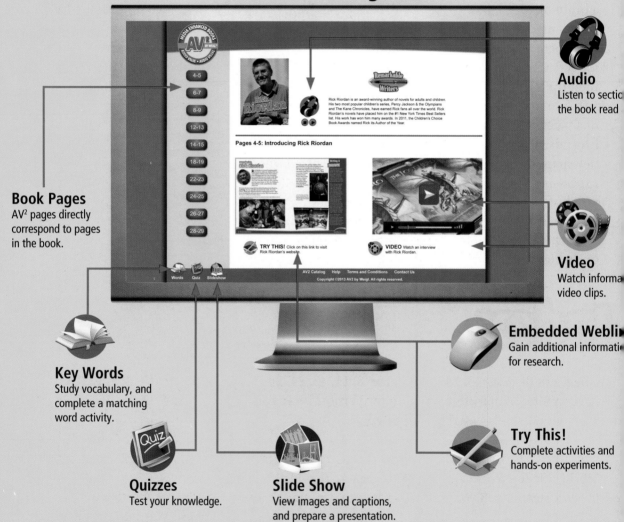

Book Pages
AV² pages directly correspond to pages in the book.

Audio
Listen to sectio the book read

Video
Watch informa video clips.

Embedded Weblir
Gain additional informatio for research.

Key Words
Study vocabulary, and complete a matching word activity.

Quizzes
Test your knowledge.

Slide Show
View images and captions, and prepare a presentation.

Try This!
Complete activities and hands-on experiments.

AV² was built to bridge the gap between print and digital. We encourage you to tell us what you like and what you want to see in the future.

Sign up to be an AV² Ambassador at www.av2books.com/ambassador.